Jail and Back

by

Cy C. Johnson

RoseDog 🐾 Books

PITTSBURGH, PENNSYLVANIA 15222

RoseDog Books
701 Smithfield Street
Pittsburgh, PA 15222
Visit our website at www.rosedogbookstore.com

ISBN: 978-1-4349-8439-5
eISBN: 978-1-4349-7430-3

Introduction

I was born the youngest of six children in the very small town of Marlin, Texas. When I was about two years old, the eight of us moved to Waco, Texas. My five siblings were much older than I. My parents were very kind to me; my family was very loving.

I had a very happy childhood. I attended the local elementary school of Oakwood Elementary. I was really blessed to attend A. J. Moore High School for a year, in my seventh grade. I later completed middle school followed by my graduation from University High School in May 1976.

After graduation, I attended Bryman Medical School of Houston, where I completed the dental assistant program. I also attended the University of Houston, where I completed the program for pre-hygiene.

Acknowledgment

This book was written to inspire someone in a special way—to see how someone like me could go through so much drama in life and live to tell the story. It took a whole lot of courage and I truly hope you are blessed. We all have choices in life and God gave us a free will that enables us to do either right or wrong. So we must always choose to do right, no matter what the cost; because bad choices will adversely affect our future.

I would like to thank my Lord and Savior Jesus Christ who inspired me to write my story. I would also like to thank Ronnie Holmes, pastor of Church of the Open Door in Waco, Texas, for patiently counseling and encouraging me during my early years as a Christian. Your ministry helped to root and ground me in God's word. Thank you! Thank you also, Gina Parker, for speaking the Lord's prophetic words to me and for meeting some of my material needs during those wilderness years. Thank you Marchelle Harris, Jennifer Lawrence, and C.M. Johnson, who shared my dream. Thank-you! Last but not least, I would like to thank my elder sister, Sander A. Taylor, for being an extraordinary sister to me. Thank-you!

Poem

Jesus I thank you for making me well
You carried me through when I fell
I will look to You for all my help
You died for me and Jesus wept.

Chapter One

My Parents

My name is Cy Charissee Johnson, but my nickname is Cookie. I will be telling you about the escapades of Cookie.

I am a very happy person. I am easily excited and have a radiant energy that is very contagious. I am a Christian. I love my Jesus, Who is my Lord and Savior.

My mother was educated, having attended Paul Quinn College of Waco. My father was a laborer who worked for Baylor University. He also worked as a custodian at night. He was a good provider.

Chapter Two

My Beginnings

I don't remember much about the small town of Marlin; but I do remember moving back there, at about age three, with my mother due to her illness. We stayed with my aunt until my mother recovered from her illness. Although I was quite young, I realized that I was not in Waco because my siblings were no longer with me. I remember feeling so homesick until my little heart was sad, very sad. I really tried to make the best of it by playing games with my older cousins.

Because of my mother's illness, I was not allowed to play with the kids next door, nor allowed to have seconds at meal times. Because of her illness, I had to do without many things.

I was around four years old when we finally moved back to Waco. Two years later, my mother took a turn for the worse and had to be hospitalized. She was diagnosed with mental illness and had to remain hospitalized for about two or three years. Although my father and siblings were still with me, my mother's absence left me feeling lonely.

Chapter Three
The Kids Next Door

The kids next door were very different—very wild and mischievous. They were always in trouble and out of control. They felt that they were always right. The older ones even tried to perform sexual acts with me. The kids next door were horrible. Even though the parents disciplined them, they were still out of control.

At six years old, I made up my mind that I would not turn out to be like the kids next door. I was not going to turn out to be a mean person.

Chapter Four

Starting Elementary School

At around six years old, I was blessed to start public school, even though my birthday came late. I received this favor because my mother had friends in high places.

I don't remember much about elementary school because that was such a long time ago, but I do remember going. I remember being embarrassed for forgetting my Christmas speech, very embarrassed.

Chapter Five

Middle School

Middle school was much different than elementary school. Here I was introduced to boys and more boys. I remember dating and falling in and out of love at the age of fourteen years old. This was one of the most special times of my life.

Bryant was the one I fell in love with. We were very close. He was kind to me and bought me many gifts, like rings, coats, and watches. We shared many things together. The fact is I was around fourteen years old when I first started smoking marijuana, better known as pot. We just started smoking it for fun. We were a very happy couple.

Chapter Six

High School

What can I say about high school? High school was challenging. It required more schoolwork and more homework. I enjoyed attending University High School. We had all types of activities going on.

I was involved in choir, even though I could not sing that well. I loved the choir. We used to put on Christmas programs for the V.A.(Veterans Administration)Hospital every year. I will never forget that I sang "Rudolph the Red-Nosed Reindeer" every Christmas. It was so much fun.

I got into trouble in high school, too. I had a fight with a bully. It was bound to happen because she thought that I was afraid of her. We were both suspended from school for three days for fighting that day. Needless to say, I never had any more problems from her.

In high school, I found an older friend, a dropout, who opened up another world for me. That world was chasing soldiers housed at the Fort Hood base in Killeen. Most of my eleventh and twelfth grade years were spent on and off in Killeen. My parents didn't think that I would graduate, but I did graduate and moved out of the house.

Chapter Seven
Moving to Houston

I moved to Houston one month after I graduated from high school, and that's when my adult life began. It was in June of 1976. I moved in with my sister Sandra in Southeast Houston. We lived in a two-bedroom apartment. I quickly became homesick. I missed home so badly; but being on my own helped me become very strong. It was a hard and cold world there, since I had no job skills. It was also very difficult to adjust on the job. I was working in a warehouse that made drapes. It was very cold in the warehouse, so I had to wear a coat all day. I missed many days as a result of the winter weather. I was completely miserable the whole time I worked there. Since I had a hard time adjusting to the jobs, my sister encouraged me to attend dental assistant school. Even though the school was expensive, I was blessed to qualify for grants and school loans.

Chapter Eight
Attending Dental Assistant School

Starting dental assistant school was a major challenge. I had to learn new medical terminology, especially all that pertained to the mouth, including glands and teeth. We were tested every other day and in order to pass, our scores needed to be high. I don't know how I did it for months, but I did it. I managed to complete the courses, graduate, and receive my diploma. I was so proud of myself.

Chapter Nine
First Job at the Dentist

I found my first job at a dentist's office through an agency. The agency placed me in an office of two African-American men, Dr. Eagleton, DDS (doctor of dental surgery) and Dr. Plummer, DDS.

My relationship with the doctors was very good. They made sure their patients were first priority. Some of my responsibilities were taking X-rays, charting, making impressions, and much more. I gained a lot of experience working in their office. In addition to having a very clean environment, the staff was excellent and very kind. My life was finally in order. I had a good job working at a dentist's office and now had my own apartment.

Things were going good in my life, until I met an old Fort Hood soldier, Paul, in Houston. I soon let him move in with me and my life began to change. We started disagreeing, arguing, and fighting. He became jealous and controlling. He started beating me. At first it was subtle, like pushing me from time to time. Then came the bruises around my eyes. No matter how hard I tried, I could not hide the bruises and redness. I later found out that he was full of drugs during the times he abused me. The abuse was so painful that it caused me to become stressed out and full of fear. I remember coming home late from the dentist's office one time, and he beat me for that. I suffered black eyes and physical problems due to the abuse. The abuse was so bad that I lost my dental assistant position and was unable to work. I had finally had enough of the abuse and got on my knees to ask God to take Paul out of my life. The Lord heard my prayer and He took him out of my life. I was around twenty years old at the time.

It's strange how women often get involved in abusive relationships. People say that women attract those kinds of men because of their father's abuse, but that's not always true; my father was never abusive.

Chapter Ten

Living in Sin

I was around twenty-one years old when I met Mr. Nice Guy, named Nelson. He worked at the railroad. I had found a new job and a new friend. He was very nice to me, but was also involved in drugs. His drug of choice was powder cocaine. I moved in with Nelson immediately. I thought that our relationship would last forever because I did drugs, too. Everything was going well between us until the phone calls started coming. It was another woman calling our home. I tried to ignore the calls, but she was very persistent. She called day and night. I even changed our phone number, hoping that this would stop the calls from coming. Somehow, she managed to get the new phone number. I was getting quite stressed out and upset by the phone calls. Since I could no longer trust Nelson, I asked him to move out of the apartment, and he did. Before he left, he purchased me some new furniture. What a nice guy.

Chapter Eleven
Living Single

I enjoyed living by myself because I was able to make my own decisions. I stopped using powder cocaine and started using pot again. I even met new friends. Marijuana was the drug of choice in the 70s. I also mixed drugs. I took Black Mollies for uppers to enjoy that high. Using drugs became a daily habit in my life. I never attended the local church. I just worked and partied. If someone had invited me to church, I would have gone. I thought that the life I was living was a good life; but I was wrong. No life without Jesus is a good life. I was partying at a local club when I met, Ray, my first husband. He seemed to be a nice, quiet man. We dated for a while and then got serious about each other.

Chapter Twelve

Horror in the Beginning of My Marriage

I was around 22 years old when I first got married. Ray was a very good man. He worked hard to provide for his family. I was also working.

One time, when I was hitchhiking to work, I was abducted by a black man in a pickup truck. When he saw me hitchhiking, he politely offered me a ride. Once I was in the vehicle, however, things changed. The man pulled out a gun and ordered me to take off all of my clothes. The gun was very large. I feared for my life! My heart was pounding and I wanted to scream out the truck window, but I was terrified that he would kill me. I was paralyzed with fear and told this stranger that I would do as he asked. I took off my sweater and said, "Be cool; I will cooperate." So he put his gun down. That gave me some relief; but my life was still in danger.

The stranger drove me to an area of some condemned houses; there were many of them. He finally came to a complete stop and got out of the truck. Then he came around to the passenger side and pulled me out. I was so nervous that I lost my balance. He grabbed my arm so that I wouldn't fall. At that time I noticed that he had no weapon to harm me. Then he walked me all the way to the back room of this condemned house. In a daze, I looked around and saw that the man had disappeared. I was wondering why he abducted me and where he had gone to. I turned and looked out the front room and what I saw still haunts me today. He had retrieved an old, nasty mattress from across the street and was dragging it to the house. So I turned and ran back to the room and jumped out the window to escape. I ran through muddy water and trees that were jungle-like. I kept on running and finally came to a tall fence and jumped over it. I immediately found a college student in a car nearby and asked him to call the police. They came and I gave them a description of the man. Then the college student took me home. I thanked God that nothing happened to me that day, because this stranger had my life in his hands. I'm so glad that I gave him the impression that I would cooperate; the result was that I was able to run and escape to my freedom. I told the story to my husband, but he did not believe me.

Chapter Thirteen
Starting a Family

Shortly after I got married, we started a family. I had a little girl and named her Tasha. She was a nice, healthy baby. I was able to stay at home and be a full-time mom for about five months. I returned to work and life quickly changed. My marriage was short-lived. My husband became withdrawn and no longer wanted to do anything. He became the most boring man alive! I still wanted to go to clubs and parties, but he did not. I would ask him to take me places, but he always refused. He never wanted to take me anywhere! After about six months of marriage, I decided to leave him. I waited until he went to work one day and moved all of my furniture and clothes out of the home we shared. He was shocked when he returned home. I think that he had emotional problems after that, for his actions indicated that he never forgave me, as though he hated me for leaving him.

Chapter Fourteen
A Single Parent

After I left my husband I began feeling very sad. I still loved him. Soon after that, I lost my job and was unemployed for a while. Being unemployed made my life bad for a while.

I finally found a job and managed to get my life back on track. Everything became all right again. The dentist I was working for was all right, the house I had was great, and my pay was outstanding. Making good money allowed me to continue partying. I partied every night and on weekends.

One day, I left my daughter with the babysitter when she was one year old. Her father went to the babysitter's house and ran off with her. He stayed in hiding with her for about six months. I was so worried and frightened. I didn't know what to do. One day, I went to church and asked God to help me find my daughter, and He did. I found her in an apartment in Houston where my husband was living with a woman. We were still married even though we were separated. When I arrived at the apartment, my husband said that our daughter wasn't there. He then pulled his motorcycle in front of my car. Now, what made him do that? For him to have done that meant trouble, if you know what I mean. I ran him over with my car while he was still on it. He got up off the ground and then got in my car. I pulled a knife out and we began to fight very fiercely. I just lost it because he had taken someone who belonged to me. I tore him up. The ambulance came and took him away. He was hospitalized and then went home. If only he had removed himself from in front of my car. Needless to say, I never had any more trouble out of him.

Chapter Fifteen
Moved to California

At the dentist's office, I met a man, Obu, from Nigeria who came to the clinic as a patient. We began talking on the phone and I found that I liked his company. After about a year, Obu invited my daughter and me to come live with him and his daughter in Los Angeles. Even though we "knew each other" for about a year, I really knew nothing about Obu except that he wanted to whisk my daughter and me off to Los Angeles. He was offering us a chance at a new life. After about six months, I accepted his offer and moved to California. My bosses at the dentist's office gave me a going-away party. Four of us were crammed into Obu's one-bedroom apartment. His daughter was age five and my daughter was age four. Shortly after we moved in, Obu and his daughter started mistreating my daughter. I felt extremely uncomfortable living there; so I started partying again. It was just the excuse that I needed to start drinking again. After all, any excuse is better than none. I began to drink every day. I decided to contact people back in Houston and also searched out and found new contacts to party with in California. I tried getting a job at a dentist's office, but they required a radiology certificate. To make matters worse, after six weeks, Obu kicked my daughter and I out of his house. He had found out that I was partying with a man in California. My daughter and I ended up in Watts Apartments, that's right, the Ghetto area. We lived there for about a week. I was still partying and hiding money in this junky house. Somehow, someone found my money and probably spent it on drugs. This made me very upset because that left me broke. That stolen money was my last 70 dollars. My ex-husband had stopped paying child support. Can you imagine the pictures I painted in my head of being totally broke? I desperately needed help. Only then did I decide to go to a church in the Watts area. I prayed to God to help send me home to Houston. He heard my cry and answered my prayers. He sent me back to a place that I called home.

Chapter Sixteen

Starting All Over Again

I called one of my co-workers back in Houston. She was a close friend. I asked her to wire me some money, and she did. My daughter and I caught the first Greyhound bus back to Houston. I remember riding that bus for many days and nights. We were broke and hungry, but we got fed. People on the bus would get off for the rest stops and bring us food each time they got off. I was so glad to make it back to Houston. Once I got back home, I was given my old job back. I had to start all over again, so I moved in with my friend. I started saving money again to move. I'm so glad that I didn't sell all my furniture before I moved to California. I stayed with my friend for about two months and then moved out.

Chapter Seventeen

A Black Cloud Came Over My Life

I had been living back in Houston for about four years when I decided to go back to school to become a hygienist. I was about twenty-eight years old at the time. If it weren't for drugs, I would be a hygienist right now. I started at University Of Houston and attended for a year. I had gone to a club and was partying like I normally do. As always, I was looking for love in all the wrong places. I had been drinking, just looking for a good time, when I met this man. He invited me to his home and, like a fool, I went. This night was the beginning of a new and evil life that I had never experienced before. I had done drugs in the past and lived through it, but this drug called crack would almost destroy my life. This is my story, living as an addict and trying to maintain a healthy balance of working and being a mother. I went to this new man's house and will never forget it. I remember riding over to his place. He made the comment that Houston was a lonely city. I really didn't think much about his comment; after all, I was used to being lonely. Once we arrived at his place, I saw a homosexual there with some crack cocaine in a big glass tube. They asked me to try some, but at first I declined. They repeatedly offered me the drug and I finally gave in and tried some. This was when all hell broke loose. I became possessed by evil spirits. I smoked for a while; then he took me home. Once I was hooked, his type of partying cost a lot of money. My life would never be the same.

Chapter Eighteen
Cocaine: A Root of All Evil

I began to lie, cheat, and steal from people to support my new habit. This habit became so overwhelming that I would stay up all night just smoking crack. School became more than I could handle, so I dropped out. Work had also become too much and I quit my job at the dentist's office.

All day, I smoked and smoked. Since I had quit working, I could not pay my rent and was kicked out. John 10:10 says, "The thief comes just to steal, kill, and destroy; but I have come that they may have life and have it abundantly."

Now I had lost everything: a chance for an education, my job, my apartment, and my self-esteem. I had allowed the devil to steal my life from me because of crack cocaine. In order to get myself back together, I had to move in with my friend, Bobbie. I don't like depending on anyone for support; but at that time, I had no other choice, because I had a child to support. Thank God she was too young to comprehend what was happening to me. Things had calmed down a little bit, but Bobbie also did drugs. So the drug demons were everywhere. Somehow, she was in control of her demons; at least, it appeared that she was. After about two weeks, my friend felt that it was time for me to get a job.

Chapter Nineteen
A New Job

Bobbie decided that I needed to work, so this time I did something different. She got me a job doing home health care. I basically did nothing all day but sit on my behind. I worked for a small, kind lady. I would bathe her and sit with her all day. I managed to stay there for about seven months. Then I decided that I needed to move out because my friend had become controlling and was acting more like a mother than a friend. After a year of living all over Houston not wanting to pay rent, I decided to move back home, to Waco, Texas, of all places. Moving back to Waco was a big mistake. We threw a big party with my friends whom I had known over the years. The party was a good going away party.

Chapter Twenty
Moved Back to Waco

I didn't know that I was pregnant when I moved back to Waco to live with my parents. That was a major change. I was back for only two weeks before I found a job with a dentist. I was so excited to get my life back on track. I still had a major problem in my life: Satan still had me bound by sin. I started my new life working at a dentist's office in Bellmead, Texas. Things were looking pretty good until the drugs appeared in the park right around the corner from my house. I went from bad to worse with the drugs. I thought that Satan had me bound in Houston. That was a drop in the bucket. The demons were super strong in Waco, back in 1988. Unbelievable! Unbelievable!

Chapter Twenty-One

I Found Out I Was Pregnant

Here I go again, back in the fast lane. I was moving real fast now. I was back in my hometown of Waco, Texas.

Right away I started feeling different, not like my normal self at all. I went and took a pregnancy test and found out I was pregnant. I told my employer about my problem, or rather, the pregnancy, and she suggested that I get an abortion. That's right, she wanted me to terminate my pregnancy. I refused to do so, because the baby was moving inside of me. I just prayed every day because I was tempted to use drugs. It is true that I used drugs off and on during my pregnancy. It was too difficult for me to stop completely at the time. Six months after I moved back, my ex-husband, Ray, decided to show up in Waco. He wanted to take my daughter back with him. At the time, my attitude was, "Who cares anyway?" He didn't want to pay child support and she was staying with my parents. I felt that, if my daughter went to live with her father, the move would result in fewer problems for me during this second pregnancy.

Finally, I gave birth to a healthy boy and named him Teddy. He was born premature, so he had to stay in the hospital for about two weeks before I took him home. By the time I took him home, he weighed five pounds. I left the hospital and started back on my drug binge. I had moved out of my parents' home, but had to move back once I had my baby. After Teddy was born, I started smoking drugs and drinking really heavy. I had plenty of drugs every day. We smoked so much that I would stay up all night. It seemed that the more I smoked, the more I wanted. The craving was nonstop. So I just kept on smoking.

After I had my son, I did not want to work at the dentist's office. It was too slow. They begged me to come back to work, but Satan had me bound so badly that the only work I could do was hustle some money to get my next fix. At the time, I did whatever it took to get some money. I stole, prostituted my body, and worked illegal jobs as much as possible. My life had been turned upside down. During this time, I ended up jumping out of a moving automobile. I jumped out of a two-story building, was raped five times and abducted once. It became a problem for my parents because I was in and out of trouble constantly. Sometimes, I would walk for days like a zombie in the streets. I looked like a living dead person. My father didn't approve of my lifestyle, but all he could do was pray for me and put up with my nonsense. He put up with my lies and stealing money from my parents to support my drug habit. It seemed that life had passed me by. Who could have known that a beautiful, successful young lady would have opened the door to such an attack on her life? Crack does not discriminate, nor is it prejudiced. It preys on the weak soul. It's a killer.

Two years had passed since I moved back to Waco. Now, at age thirty-two, I began focusing more on my son.

Chapter Twenty-Two
A Problem

Now that I was focusing on Teddy, I began to notice that he was having trouble walking, although he was already two years old. Something was definitely wrong, because he was walking strangely. I took him to the doctor and he diagnosed Teddy with cerebral palsy due to his premature birth. It seemed that his right leg was shorter than his left. Just like my father, the same leg. What a coincidence. At age two, Teddy was fitted with some ugly brown shoes to support his standing and walking. By age five, his right leg was at least three inches shorter than his left one.

Chapter Twenty-Three
Life Passes You By

I was living a life of hell here on earth, chasing drugs day after day and night after night. It was the year 1993 and time had passed very quickly. I hardly recognized myself. I was so skinny, my hair looked bad, and my skin color had become really black, like coal. This was okay with me, because in my mind, I was still sexy and attractive. Of course, this impression was only in my mind. When you're deep into drugs, you don't want to take care yourself, much less think about hygiene. I was taking very few baths because I didn't have time. Things got worse in September. My father passed away in the nursing home due to an asthma attack. I was unable to care for both of my parents, so they had to go to in a nursing home one by one. I wasn't able to take care of my son either. I had to enlist the help of a friend of mine. She took care of Teddy most of the time. I couldn't, because I was too busy chasing drugs to be worried about him.

Meanwhile, I was getting deeper and deeper into trouble in the streets. The first set of charges that the law brought against me was for criminal trespassing. They placed me on probation. I was still running the streets like a mad woman and getting high on crack. The second set of charges was for prostitution, which was a violation of probation. Jail time was coming. I convinced the judge that I would be willing to do weekends only and he agreed to it. But every weekend, before I turned myself in, I would drink heavily. The jailer had told me that I had to stop drinking before I could turn myself in, so from the second weekend on, I decreased the amount of alcohol that I drank before turning myself in. Finally, I completed my jail sentence. I was free to run the streets once again.

Chapter Twenty-Four
Doing Time

Another year had passed and it was now 1994. I was a drug addict living only for drugs and alcohol. I had become my own worst nightmare. By April, I was sick and tired of the party life. I decreased my own intake of drugs and stopped the drug dealers from coming to my house to sell drugs. One month after I began to turn my life around, the police caught up with my past crimes.

I'll never forget 1994, because it was the year when I was arrested for three charges of selling crack. Can you imagine how I felt, having these drug charges on my record at the age of thirty-six years old? I should have turned my life around by now. I should have stopped doing drugs and settled down and enjoyed life to the fullest. But no, I wanted the fast life of sex and drugs everyday. I had low self-esteem and no dignity. I was just a sad, fearful, hopeless being. It was in May when the police finally caught up with me. They found me walking in front of Oakwood Park when they arrested me and threw me into jail for the three counts of selling crack. And guess what? All of my party friends were nowhere to be found. They didn't even come to see me while I was in jail. They no longer had time for me, because of my environment (jail). I now had to live by a new set of rules here in jail.

While sitting in jail facing so many charges, I became afraid and felt all alone. I felt cold inside. I had never felt so cold and sad in all my life. I could only ask, why me? Why me, when I was trying to change my life? I was getting what I deserved. After all, I had lived like hell and never cared for anything but drugs and more drugs. For seven years, the only thing I had been living for was drugs. Now, there were no more drugs, no more parties, and no more sex—no more of anything that I had placed importance on. Before being in jail, I didn't like myself. Now, in jail, I came to hate myself. I didn't like anyone at the time. I had to adjust to being locked up like an animal. As I reflected back on my life, I realized that God had saved me—because I could have died. I could have killed myself with drug overdoses or could have been killed after

I was raped. I still remember that night as though it were yesterday. I had just made some money and was getting out of the car at a deserted area in southeast Houston. Suddenly, a man whom I hardly knew came up and grabbed me. He wanted to have sex with me, so I yanked myself free from his grip and ran to the nearby bus stop. I begged the people there to help me, because this man was trying to rape me. It was dark and they all seemed to be in a daze. They made no response to my pleas. Then the man came up to us and told the people that I was his wife. Then he hauled me off to a dark area, pulled out a knife, and threatened to rape me. Even though I was afraid, I told him to put his knife down and he did. He raped me, but did not take my life. He told me that the only reason he didn't kill me was because he knew that I had a son.

Chapter Twenty-Five
Becoming a Christian

Now God had my attention. He could finally reach me. He had saved my soul and saved my life. When I was in the world, I was slowly killing myself; but now I could live for God and read the Bible. I knew that it was going to be hard at first, because I was a baby Christian. I had asked Jesus into my life and He saved me. I knew that I had many challenges ahead of me and many obstacles to climb, but I had Jesus with me.

As of May 1994, I was in jail. I didn't like it; I didn't like it at all. "Please, God, get me out of this place," I kept praying. "I'll be good; I'll change my wicked ways. God, please get me out of here, because I don't belong in here. I'll be good, God. Just give me one more chance, please." But *no*! I had to remain in jail with these bad people, so to speak. I guess I had made my bed, but I didn't want to lie in it. It was in lockup. I didn't like this bed at all!

I had first given my life to the Lord before my first misdemeanor charges, in 1993. Now He had saved me once again. Some people would call this Jail House Religion, but I call it peace, joy, and love. I had found Jesus again and He was on my side now. I was still afraid, because I would still be sent to prison this time. I had been arrested before, but those charges were for misdemeanors. The charges I was now facing were felonies. That meant that I was being sent to prison on some serious charges. I had told some undercover officers where to buy some crack. Now, because of their entrapment schemes, I was facing three felony charges. "There should be some law against their laws for entrapment," I kept thinking. "Dirty rats! They're all rats!" All I wanted to do was party everyday and support my habit; this was what my life in Waco had become. It's true that the police had set me up. But God used the entrapment and subsequent jail time to shake me up and get my life back on track.

Very early during my jail time, I figured that I would be all right because I was still alive. I decided that I had better make the most of a bad situation.

But I was still feeling angry and bitter over all that had happened. One of my "road dogs" (best friend) received only one felony charge. I believe that they had me confused with her because she looked just like me. Even the people at the white clubs always mistook her for me. I felt that she should have been given the three felony charges that I had received, because she rode with the undercover cops more than I did. I believe that they gave me her charges and she received mine. I had yet to find out the consequences for the three felonies.

After four months, I had my court date. They gave me fifteen years. "That was too many years for such a little thing!" I thought. I felt that they didn't like me because I was a drug addict. "God, why so many years? Why me?" I was in shock for the rest of the day. I kept praying, "God, please help me to get a hold of myself!" They say "Don't do the crime if you can't do the time." That's an understatement. I didn't ever want to do anything wrong again! I was going to change my life. I was now going to live for Jesus Christ, my Lord and Savior.

After serving seven months in the county jail, I was now on my way to the Big House. I had never been to prison before and didn't know what to expect. "But come what may," I prayed, "I'm going to continue to walk with You, Jesus. Because I know that everything will be all right as long as You are with me. After all, You have kept me safe from harm." My constant prayer became, "Jesus, I am Yours; have Your way with me."

I had made up my mind; I was determined to follow Jesus no matter what.

Chapter Twenty-Six
Pulling Chain

First, let me tell you how good God is. The following information was given to me by a fellow prisoner. I cannot remember a thing about pulling chain. The following is a description of a personal friend. I am letting you know of the things that God completely wiped out of my remembrance.

This is when you are being transported to TDC (Texas Department of Corrections). You are taken through the process of classification to determine which prison unit you will be sent to. The process consists of health, physical, and mental checks with doctors and psychologists. They also check for age and crime history. First, you get a blood test, shots, and hearing and eye exams. They then check to see if you are suicidal or mentally competent and able to adjust to prison life. This whole process takes up to eight weeks, and it is pure hell! They also take additional pictures, fingerprints and a record of all tattoos and any and all identifying scars. You have to stand in a line naked until it's your turn to be seen and get talked to like you're a piece of trash! Each day, a different process is done and you eat sack lunches called "Johnnies" during the process. This process takes so long because there are so many of us being processed and classified. Once you have completed this process, you go before a committee and get told which unit you will be placed in.

Now, I just had to wait until I got called out in the night to go to my assigned prison unit. Until then, I had to wait in a holding cell until the bus got there. Once this happened, I arrived about 2 A.M. to my assigned unit. Once I arrived, I had to endure more medical tests and go before my unit prison warden to receive from him my job assignment. From then on, I was doing my time in pure hell. This was the consequence of my mistakes and poor choices I made while in the society. I must also remember that to gain parole was a privilege, not a right; at least, this was what I was told. My life was no longer my own, they told me; I was just job security to them.

I had now become a number and was no longer a person.

Chapter Twenty-Seven
Prison Population

You are assigned a cellblock or dorm, whichever, to determine your custody level. When you first go in, all eyes are on you and your belongings. Prison bullies and homosexuals size you up as you go to your cell. Once you arrive, you will have to make your bed and meet your new cell-mate. Once this task is completed, you are taken to the day room to meet and greet your fellow inmates. Most new inmates look around to see if there is anyone they may know. Many of the inmates will ask you a lot of questions, such as "Where you are from?" and "How much time do you have?" The main goal is to stay to oneself and just blend in, *not fit in*. You have to remember you can also lose your life there, too. You mostly learn to make wise choices because your freedom and life depend on it. The next morning, you go eat breakfast (called chow) and find out where your meals will be and then go to your assigned job. Your best bet is to adjust to prison life A.S.A.P. (as soon as possible) and do your time and not someone else's. You must stay out of all scams and hustling. You must write your family and tell them where you are. You must have someone to write to on the outside of prison to maintain a sense of balance. Prison food is horrible, but sustainable. It will keep you alive to work another day, as they say. It is always good if you can keep some commissary in your locker box. This will tide you over until the next day. Another rule of thumb is that you must always remember to never borrow or lend anything in prison. This could be costly. The time sheets were sent to us through the mail and our parole status was on it. My saving grace was the Lord Jesus Christ and reading the Bible. Outside of sustaining me spiritually, it kept many of the other prisoners away. It also kept me from associating with the bad crowd and helped me prepare for the outside.

Chapter Twenty-Eight
My New Cellmate

I would not wish prison on anyone. I arrived there in January of 1995. This was my new home now and I didn't like it at all. I didn't like my cellmate either. She was an older, mean lady. She would wake me up at night and tell me to roll over because she claimed I had been snoring. I did not like to be woken up. She seemed to think she knew the whole Bible, but she did not. She also talked too much and believed she was all that and a bag of chips. Boy, was she wrong. She had been locked up a long time; I think that she had Jail House Religion. Anyway, I was there now and had to make the best of it. I felt I had to respect her because she was my elder. God Bless her.

They gave me a new job in the prison, and I didn't like it because it was called the hoe squad. So I had to fill out a form to get a new job; I did and it worked. I got a new job working in the laundry and liked this job.

Chapter Twenty-Nine
Church Activities

After a year in prison, I was starting to have a good relationship with God. By this time, I was involved in many church activities. My walk with Jesus was good; God is good! "Oh taste and see that the Lord is good, blessed is the man that trusts in Him" (Psalm 34:8). The volunteers who came to visit were awesome! There is a Scripture that says, "When I was hungry you fed Me, when I was sick you visited Me…. I tell you the truth, when you did this for these, even the least of My brothers, you did it unto Me." (Matt. 25:35-36, 40) I am truly glad that Christian people take time out of their daily lives to come and share the Word of God. For Matthew 28:19 says, "Go ye therefore and teach all nations, baptizing them in the name of the Father and Son and of the Holy Ghost."

Chapter Thirty

Bad News

I had been in prison for about a year when I received word that my mother had died. This was very disturbing news; even worse was the fact that I could not go to her funeral. I was unable to attend my own mother's funeral. I felt cold and sad inside, totally alone. I really needed a touch from the Lord, because I had sunk to the very pit of hell. I called on the Lord to carry me through this storm, this storm of grief. Psalm 91 says, "Because he hath set his love upon Me, therefore I will deliver him. I will set him on high, because he hath known My name. He shall call upon me and I will answer him. I will be with him in trouble; I will deliver him and honour him. With long life will I satisfy him and show him My salvation." Believe me when I say that the Lord is so very good. I only went through a three-day grieving period; I remember this so vividly.

I had now been in prison for two years. I received visits from my family from time to time, which really helped. I overheard someone talking while I was in the pill line, and from then on, I was able to get in touch with my daughter. I was asking the Lord to help me get through this crisis, and He had been faithful to do so. I can remember attending church activities and felt like I was walking on a cloud, because the presence of the Holy Spirit is very, very strong in prisons. That's right!

While in prison, I found out I that had high blood pressure. I could have died had it not been for the Lord. Now, in prison, I was walking, praying, reading my Bible, and taking my medication for high blood pressure. I had other medical problems that I was also being treated for, but they were minor.

After I had been there a year, they changed the procedure for our cell doors. When we remained in our cells, the doors closed tight and you couldn't get out; all you could do was read your Bible. Your roommates were sometimes nice and sometimes mean. You never knew what to expect. After being in prison for three years, I was ready for a change in jobs. I had grown tired of counting clothes and tired of being counted. It was time for me to make a change. After all, I didn't like being in prison anyway; but I had learned to adjust. They promoted me to status 2, which is a trustee's status. I did light sweeping and cleaned bathrooms. It was a very easy job and I was not locked up in a cell. Instead, they put us in cubicles. We were able to move around until bedtime. It was a little better, but after surviving three years in prison, I was ready to go.

My relationship with Jesus had given me patience to endure the pain and pressure that the enemy threw my way. I had learned to stand up and sit down. I had learned when to keep my mouth shut and when to voice my opinion. "I can do all things through Christ, Who strengthens me" (Philippians 4:13). I was ready to leave this place!

I now had to wear glasses prescribed by the optometrist. They were working well; but they were ugly and black.

My relationship with the Lord grew intimate. With each passing day, I came to know Him better and better as my Lord and Savior. He spoke to my spirit man. I could hear His quiet, still voice. I was feeling very good about myself because I had come such a long way with Christ. I could have been dead, but God said "No" to the devil. He said, "This one is Mine." I will always love the Lord for that, because He loved me when I didn't even love myself. Even when I tried to kill myself with drugs and alcohol, God loved me. He loves me unconditionally. He loved me *before* I loved myself. John 3:16 says, "For God so loved the world that He gave His only begotten Son, that whosoever believeth in Him should not perish but have everlasting life." That was my comfort in this cold and miserable place. It was now time for me to go home and take the Lord with me. Some people may call it Jail House Religion, but I call it hope. My hope is in Jesus.

Chapter Thirty-One
Going Home

I was on my way home now and was so excited. I could hardly wait; it was time to get free from the bars that had been keeping me bound. I was free from the demons that attacked me when I was weak; free from the constant roll calls and the dorm counts every day. No more sounding of the cell doors closing, which was enough to break you. Oh, but Jesus kept me safe and out of harm's way. He kept me safe and free inside. He gave me hope when there was none and peace where there was no peace. He kept me alive!! Now, I could go and tell the story of my prison life. I was going home to my son who was now about nine years old, going on ten. That was the hardest part of my prison time, being away from my Teddy. Now, I could be the mother that God had called and meant for me to be.

I was afraid to be on my own. I was home and was trying to adjust to being back in society. It was a little difficult at first; but Jesus was there with me wherever I went. I decided to attend a local church. I called them up and they provided me with transportation. I was able to attend church regularly and it was a great feeling, just being able to freely worship God with peace of mind.

One thing I really did not like about being out of prison was people asking me how long I had been out. They continued to ask over and over. I guess that's all they could think of to say. Bless their hearts.

Chapter Thirty-Two
My First Job Out

I soon got my first job and was so excited to be working and making money. I was happy that I could now save money and get my own place. I really needed to feel independent. I was doing great now. I soon got two more jobs. I was just working and saving money and it was a wonderful feeling. Everything was going just fine until I took my eyes off of Jesus. I found a college student, Otis, who appealed to me. It had only been three months since my release and I was starting to fall back into sin. John 10:10 says, "The thief cometh not but for to steal, and to kill and destroy; I come that they might have life and that they have it more abundantly." The enemy knows our weaknesses and he knows just how to bring the wrong person into our life and make that person look very appealing.

Like a fool, I took the bait. This led me down the road of destruction yet again, because I took my eyes off the prize (Jesus). Once again, I found myself in bondage. I had become a prisoner in my mind because the enemy had bound me in sin again.

This man I met was bound with evil spirits that I was at first unaware of. He had the demon of alcohol. This evil spirit hid itself from me very well. I could not see it; he appeared normal. The man looked cute and had a nice smile; but I was trying to make a relationship that was all wrong for me work, and I was still blind. I began living in sin again. The reason I decided to live in sin was because of fear, a paralyzing fear of failure. The enemy had told me that I needed a roommate, and I fell for it. He had managed to trick me once again. Now I was living with an alcoholic and I began drinking, too.

The best thing about God is that He looks at your insides and not your outside. He sees your internal and spiritual changes, while the world still sees you as an addict. Many will say, "Once an addict always an addict." They can be cruel about the things they say about you and the way they treat you. People will accuse you of things you have not done. They will accuse you of being somewhere you were not, trying to let you know that they are watching you, just waiting for you to fail. These are the people who really don't care. My dad always told me that some people love to talk and tell lies.

Chapter Thirty-Three
Old Habits Will Repeat Themselves

I fell back into my old habits. That's right, God had set me free of all demons and now all of them were back. The Bible tells us that once you've been set free of evil spirits, they go. But, then they come back to see if your house is clean, and my house was open for unclean spirits. So they brought seven more with them. You can be sure that I was in real trouble right about now, and the church was warning me not to go back to Egypt; but I would not listen. I became the ugly duck, because sin makes you look ugly. I had been a walking testimony; but now I had become a walking disaster once again. Since I was working three jobs now, I justified everything that I did. I started moving from place to place, relationship to relationship, still in sin.

My monthly income was large and I was blowing it all on drugs. What a mess all over again! You would think that I had learned my lesson by now, but Satan had me bound to drugs and alcohol once again. These men were all so stupid and I was stupid! This life was a nightmare. I didn't like myself anymore; I needed help. The Lord heard me and sent help. I didn't get clean right away; it was a process. I knew that I must first be honest and sincere. Instead of using my money to buy drugs and alcohol, I began sending money to different churches and asking them pray for my weaknesses. I had to believe in myself enough to cry out to God to save me, and He did. It was a very difficult process and took over a year.

Chapter Thirty-Four (a)
Preparation for Recovery

At this time, I was living like a racehorse and still on parole. The parole officer had no idea what to do with me or what to think of me. I still managed to continue with my drug use. I had been getting high for the previous year; that's a lot of drugs! I should have been ashamed of myself, but a drug addict does not care. They care only about getting more drugs.

But I had asked the Lord to set me free from drugs and alcohol. After a whole year, I still struggled with addiction. I was attending meetings and therapy every day. I was so sick and tired of being sick and tired. The drugs kept coming my way. The more I was committed to quit, the more drugs the devil sent my way. I was now at a point when I couldn't get any higher. I was wasting my life away. My son was completely aware of what was going on and he did not say a thing to me. He kept quiet, like a good little boy. For no other reason but him, I was going to get off these stupid drugs—for my son. I loved my son so much and no matter what it took, I was going to get clean and get off these drugs. This addiction was slowly killing me, like committing suicide. Anyone who does drugs does not love himself. I loved myself; now the steps to recovery could begin.

Chapter Thirty-Four (b)
Making a Change

Love for my son greatly motivated me to get clean. However, the cops were also a great motivation to get clean. I was so tired of being stopped, picked up, and let lose by the cops. I knew that I belonged to Jesus Christ. I was sick and tired of being sick and tired. I desperately needed help. I needed to help myself. I needed to "resist the devil and he will flee" (James 4:7).

Chapter Thirty-Four (c)
Recovery Is a Process

My participation in the twelve-step recovery program was not by choice; it was mandated by my parole officer. I trusted Jesus to deliver me out of my mental addiction. I needed to be delivered from guilt, paranoia, shame, depression, self-consciousness, and foolishness. I believed that Jesus Christ was my Lord and Savior, that He died on the cross for all my sins (John 3:16) and that through Him I had everlasting life. So I chose life through Jesus Christ, my Lord and Savior. Now, it was time to *live* this truth and I knew that it was not going to be easy because I did not get on the path of sin overnight. I just had to take recovery one day at a time. It's a process!

"The thief comes to steal, kill and destroy; I come that they might have life, and that they might have it more abundantly" (John 10:10). I was not going to let the thief steal from me anymore. I was on my way to recovery once again. Amen! I was still on parole and they had really been giving me a hard time because of dirty UAs (urinalyses). My urinalyses were dirty! Too dirty!

Chapter Thirty-Five (a)
The Recovery Program

The program works for those who will work it, because it teaches us a lot of things about ourselves. Those of us who did not die of disease would go off to prison, mental institutions, or complete demoralization as the disease progressed.

Drugs and alcohol had given us the feeling that we could handle whatever situation might develop. We became aware, however, that drug and alcohol usage was largely responsible for some of our worst predicaments. Some of us could spend the rest of our lives in jail for a drug-related crime.

We became enslaved to our addiction and prisoners of our own mind. We had to reach our own rock bottom before we were willing to stop. We were finally motivated to seek help in the latter stages of our addiction.

Chapter Thirty-Five (b)

My Recovery

I attended a drug rehabilitation program that dealt with the mind, will, and emotions. I had come to the point in my life that I had to change my stinky thinking.

I had a lot of problems in my past during my parole because I kept on turning in dirty UAs. I had managed to get through parole without being put on a monitor or being sent back to prison. "But enough is enough!" I decided.

Thank God I chose to work on this part of my life. There was room for change. I had no transportation but did have a job.

I had to take part in a five-days-a-week treatment program until there was a sign of improvement. At this time, I had no transportation and had no choice but to take the city bus to and from the meetings. To become successful in the treatment program, I had to take one day at time. When the parole officer said that I needed treatment, I thought that they would treat the body, not the mind. Boy, was I in for a surprise! We had to turn in form after form regarding questions about how I became an addict.

I did not like the program because it was two hours a day and I felt that I needed only one hour a day. There were also other reasons why I did not like the program, but I attended them no matter what. I wanted to get clean and stay clean. There are some things in life that require sacrifice, especially if you want them to work on your behalf.

Being clean and sober was and still is a choice for me. I had to make a choice to stay clean and sober, no matter what it took. Everyday, I had to say to myself, "I will not use drugs and alcohol." It is a must that you believe what you say, no matter what. This means that no matter how you are feeling or what you are thinking, you will not give in. If you begin to feel weak that day, you must call on the Lord. If this doesn't work, call a Christian to pray for you, or contact your sponsor.

Chapter Thirty-Five (c)
A Bad Relationship

Just like that, I fell back into sin! I allowed Mike, a drug addict, into my life. Of course, I did not think that he was addicted; after all, he looked normal to me and was going to church. I thought he was a born-again Christian, but he was not. Here I went again, looking for love in all the right places (church), but it was not the right time.

My flesh told me that I was lonely and ready to date. This was the wrong thought process. Since I was in the early stages of sobriety, I was not ready for a relationship. I chose not to listen to the truth. I started listening to my fleshly desire, got involved with a man whom I barely knew, and started falling into temptation and sin. James 1:13-14 says, "Let no man say when he is tempted, I am tempted of God: for God cannot be tempted with evil, neither tempteth He any man; but every man is tempted, when he is drawn away of his own lust, and enticed."

That relationship turned out to be a bummer! This man had been battling drugs and alcohol for most of his life and had been in and out of prison. I sure can pick them, can't I! After all, the man looked real good and real young—much younger than me!

The Bible says, "Place a guard over your heart" (Prov. 4:23). And once again I fell! I had been clean for months and then let Mike move into my home, not knowing that he had many demons attached to him. After he moved in, he told me that he smoked drugs and enticed me to join him. Satan comes to kill, steal, and destroy (John 10:10).

I had allowed this person into my life and he brought me down. I started using drugs again and now my life was in trouble. Thank God that I didn't continue in this madness, this bad relationship. I was still in treatment, so I told my counselor about the man I had met and that he had enticed me to do drugs. She did not think that was a good reason to do drugs. She let me have it in the classes! All my classmates came down on me. They were telling me that I should have said no. I was a little disappointed but soon got over it because I knew that they were right. I should have been stronger and should have said no to both the man and the drugs.

Now that I had kicked him to the curb along with the drug called crack, I could pursue sobriety again. I could stop looking to men to meet my needs and look to God, Who always provides. Philippians 4:19 says, "But my God shall supply all your needs according to His riches in glory by Christ Jesus."

Chapter Thirty-Five (d)
What Is an Addict?

What drove me to become an addict? I couldn't answer those questions at the time, but I can now. To me, an addict is a person who doesn't like himself or herself. Drug addicts hate themselves, and for this reason, they poison themselves. They have low self-esteem and the stresses of life attribute to their drug use. They just don't care.

I was learning this in the program. It was helping me to deal with the problems and issues of my mind, one day at a time. The program gave me all the help I needed and I gave my all in return. It took me one year with the help of the Lord, who was with me every step of the way.

Chapter Thirty-Six (a)
A New Me

I began my new life clean and sober, which was very different for me. You see, I now had to change people, places, and things. In other words, I had to move out of my old neighborhood and make new friends in a new environment. My former addict friends had no idea where I would be moving to.

Chapter Thirty-Six (b)
Putting Christ First

Everything started to work out. I began attending church regularly. The thief comes to kill, steal, and destroy (John 10:10). I didn't allow the enemy to steal this Scripture from my spirit. I positioned myself around positive, faith-filled Christians. I made Jesus Christ my Lord and Savior and put Him first in my life. Once again, Matt 6:33 says, "Seek first the kingdom of God and His righteousness and all things shall be given unto you."

Beginning my life as a clean and sober Christian was hard at first, because I had spent so many years trying to be the best in a sinful world. I had been looking for love in all the wrong places, which caused me to fall into sin. Now, I was looking for love in all the right places, which was the Lord Jesus Christ!

Chapter Thirty-Seven
The New, Clean Me

Prior to becoming clean and sober, being clean was not important to me. Now that I had become clean and sober, I found that I like all things to be clean and in order around me. While still in my old apartment, I purchased a brand new bedroom suite and developed a new credit line at a local furniture store. This was a great improvement over my past. I was working and saving money to buy a car. Previously, I was not capable of saving money because of the drugs, but this changed.

Now that I was allowing Jesus to be the head, He was helping me stay clean and sober and to manage my money. After a few months of being sober and drug free, I became a little too confident and felt that I was ready to handle a relationship. A recovering addict really needs to be clean for at least a year before starting a relationship. I started seeking for someone to begin a relationship with; but God was merciful and prevented any man from coming to entice me.

The Bible tells us to place a guard around our hearts (Prov. 4:23). I soon took that Scripture to include that I must protect my sobriety and stay focused on the living Word of God.

Chapter Thirty-Eight
A New Creation in Christ

Staying clean and sober is a process because it happens one day at a time. Some days may seem hard for a recovering addict. I knew that when hard times come, I could call on Jesus and He would hear my cry!

I was happy to be a new person in Christ. In 2 Corinthians 5:17, it says, "Therefore if any man be in Christ, he is a new creature: old things are passed away; behold, all things are become new." This was me; I was a new creature in Christ and the old had passed away. I knew that I must occupy my time daily.

Now that I was a new creation in Christ, I was going to have to change some things, such as my surroundings. The first change was the new bedroom suite; but I also had to move to a new location. I knew that I had changed, but the drug addicts and drug dealers didn't care; nor did they believe that I had changed. They were still coming to my old place and knocking at my door at all hours of the night. I would tell them that I had changed and no longer did drugs, but they refused to believe me. I was so tired of this madness. I had to move! The old apartment was not in the best condition. The city of Waco had put a green tag on the whole apartment complex. Under these circumstances, we were given the opportunity to relocate to new surroundings. Of course, at the time, I viewed this event as a misfortune. But the Lord worked it out for good, because He took me out of my old apartment and put me in another place. No one knew where I had moved to. Thus I was able to break free from the drug world. So what I viewed as a misfortune (the city green tagging the old apartment), God turned into a blessing.

Chapter Thirty-Nine
Restored Relationships

I now moved out of that dump of an apartment. The owners of that apartment didn't believe in exterminators and acted as though they had never heard of the word. Now that I moved into a new apartment, everything was so nice and clean.

I could have destroyed my life with the drugs and alcohol, but thank God, He gave me another chance. He allowed me to change my living habits! I knew that I must continue to go to church and read my Bible every day. I got a new vehicle and it sure felt great. Being a car owner gave me a wonderful sense of independence. I didn't have to catch a bus anymore. I also found out a lot about myself. I found myself enjoying my own company, now that I was clean and sober, and no longer wanting to be around a lot of people. I was so happy to be by myself, especially knowing that the Lord was watching over me each and every day.

I now enjoyed going to church most of the time. I loved to look nice and neat all of the time. I also loved getting my hair and nails done. I now knew how to love and take care of myself. The best part was that I now had a good relationship with my son, Teddy. Now that I was able to remain drug and alcohol free, we got along just fine. Also, the relationship with my daughter had become awesome. She called me momma even though I did not raise her. This was definitely a God thing! My daughter is a warm, beautiful young lady, whom I am very proud to call mine. God has been awesome to my daughter and me! He preserved our relationship through many ups and downs we have had. We're still very close, thanks to God!

The weather was so beautiful on this day. The sun was shining brightly. I had regained a love for clothes and dressing up. I had lost this feeling. Satan had bound me up so deeply in drugs that I did not know left from right or if I was coming or going. I had lost the feeling of loving myself enough to dress up. In the book of Isaiah, it says: "But the wicked are like the troubled sea, when it cannot rest, whose waters cast up mire and dirt. There is no peace, says my God, for the wicked" (Isaiah 57:20-21).

Every day became a holiday to me because I didn't need an excuse to party or celebrate. I lived to party or celebrate. I was the living dead party girl, but Jesus came into my life and set me free. Thank God for Calvary. The Bible says that once you are set free, you are free indeed! My spirit is free indeed.

Chapter Forty
Freedom in Christ

Now I was finally on the right track to freedom in Christ because I had moved to a new location. Nobody knew me in the new place. My new life had begun with a clean start. I was still attending all my classes at the rehab center for addicts. The first step to recovery is to admit that you have a problem and then comes delivery. This program teaches that once an addict always an addict; but the Bible tells us that once you are set free, you are free indeed! So I chose to believe the Bible. I'm a new creature in Christ and the old things have passed away, like the drugs, alcohol, and cigarettes. Now new things were taking place in my life, like church activities, and it felt so good to be free.

Chapter Forty-One
Finished the Program

It was January of 2002, and I was finally finished with the drug program. I served one full year, a long time. I don't ever want to go through that again. It's too much time and paperwork, not to mention the classes. It was worth it. Thank God for rehabilitation.

During those times, I sowed seeds into different ministries while enduring the devil's attacks. Some people in these ministries prayed for me and for my recovery. I would often be down to my last $10.00 but, instead of calling the drug dealers, I would send the money to a minister to pray for me.

However, it takes some people longer than others. Some end up relapsing and going back; not me. I didn't like attending Alcoholics Anonymous (A.A.) meetings. They were so boring. They all acted as though they were big shots in the meetings. But they were simply alcoholics and very, very boring.

I attended many of the Narcotics Anonymous (N.A.) meetings. They were always full of too much cursing; in fact, everything that came out of their mouths was a curse word and that made me feel very uncomfortable. I never liked attending these meetings, but I had to because they were required; therefore, I attended. Don't get me wrong about those meetings, I mean some meetings were exciting to be in, but some were boring. All in all, I managed to stay clean and sober. After one year of attending meetings, I was ready to put God in first place in my life. I decided to make Him the center of my life at all costs. Once my mind was made up, I started attending church services all over again. With a new, clean, and sober life, I started going to church every time their doors were open.

Chapter Forty-Two
My New Life

I moved into a new apartment and now had a job as a waitress in Golden Coral. Waiting tables was a challenge, but it paid the bills. My God always supplied all my needs according to 4:19).

I continued to serve God and stay clean and sober. I enjoyed every bit of it; but of course, life always has its challenges. For instance, now that I was clean and sober, people looked at me differently. They acted as though it was a great surprise that I cleaned up my life and was no longer involved in drugs. They would make statements such as, "I didn't know you weren't on drugs anymore," and ask stupid questions such as "Where have you been?" I just looked at them and said, "I stopped using drugs years ago!" But they were still amazed and wanted to know how and when I stopped using drugs. What surprised me was that some of the people who asked these questions or made these statements had also been prior drug users and had been able to quit. It amazed me that they could accept their own triumph over drugs but not believe that someone like me could have the same victory. Nevertheless, I still acted very nice and shined as usual.

I was no longer attending the drug rehab program; I just attended NA meetings and church. I was a single parent working and taking good care of my son, who had become my focus in life. I must remember that children remember almost everything; they forget very little.

Chapter Forty-Three
My Son

I was proud of my son, Teddy, because he was born with cerebral palsy and had to face many challenges early in his life. Most of his peers made fun of him during his early years because of his disabilities. He was also diagnosed with ADD (attention deficit disorder), but glory to God, we continued to act on the Word of God and my son continued to improve. Finally, during his freshman year in high school, we were able to take him completely off the medication.

Because the cerebral palsy prevented his right leg from growing, Teddy underwent three surgeries to correct the tendons in his leg, knee, and ankle. The surgeries consisted of stretching the tendons so that both of his legs could be as equal to each other in length as possible. His third and last surgery, in his junior year in high school, was truly successful, because he was then able to put his weight equally on both legs. He was able to stand and walk straight. God is so good and Teddy looked absolutely great. He had a great disposition in spite of his differences. He stands six feet tall and is very handsome. I believe that we all have some type of a handicap, whether it is visible or invisible. I say this because, apart from God, we cannot do anything; we are handicapped. Without God, we are unable to walk with dignity and act with integrity. *With* God, we are complete. God peels off of us old, selfish, worldly habits and makes us complete in Him. "I can do all thing through Christ, which strengthens me (Philippians 4:13).

My son has made me so proud. Teddy is a good person and very intelligent. In spite of his condition, he graduated from high school and soon started college as a business major. He runs the sound system for the U-Turn Church and participates in their activities. It looks like he is following in his mamma's footsteps in being active in church. I am so proud of him. I pray that he keeps up the great work.

Speaking of church ministries, I am and have been a discipler for many years. This involves calling and praying for people as needed.

I believe that God has a reason for everything, including blessing us with success and a good clean life. I'm grateful that God chose me out of all my old drug addict friends to clean up my life. I believe that He can do it for you. No matter what you may be going through, God is the answer for your success. No matter what trial or tribulation you may be facing in your life today, God is the answer. "Seek first the kingdom of God and His righteousness and all things will be given to you" (Matthew 6:33), things such as a good job, a home, a car, whatever you need. God is the answer to your success! No man can ever bring you success, but Jesus our Lord and Savior can.

Chapter Forty-Four

Second Marriage

I was around forty-four years old when I met a man, named Lee, at church. He seemed to be interesting and was much younger than me. I felt that it was about time to start dating, I now know that this was true. Lee looked like my type and he seemed to like me as well. To make a long story short, we began dating. Then, when I was forty-seven years old, we got married. My husband, Lee, was very quiet and shy. He is a Dallas man and one of the youngest siblings in his family. It wasn't love at first sight. We fought a whole lot, almost all the time. In so many ways, we were totally different. We had different values about life, too. Our personalities were also very different. Lee was an introvert and I was an extrovert.

My life changed once again. I was married but still very committed to Jesus. I was still very actively serving in church. When I was facing problems, I was sometimes unwilling to serve in church. I soon discovered, however, that this is the most perfect time to serve, when we are facing trials and tribulation. Satan is a busy evil spirit, and when you think that you have it all together and decide to relax, that's when he comes in like a flood. So stay prayed up at all times. The Bible tells us to stay in prayer all the time.

Chapter Forty-Five
A Brand-New Home

Now, I was forty-eight years old and Jesus had been with me throughout my life. I waited tables to be blessed, to make ends meet. My job was difficult at times because of its demands. For instance, there were many different types of people who came to eat at the restaurant. Some were nice and some were rude and nasty. I tried to make all my customers as comfortable as possible and kept a big smile on my face at all times. I found that a lot of people love to talk, and I sometimes got caught up in a conversation, which put me behind in my work. I tried to keep my talking to a minimum. We didn't have a busboy, so I was responsible for busing all my tables as well as refilling drinks. I did a lot of walking. Now that I was attending classes to become a new homeowner, I got to sit down in class. What a relief. The classes took two hours a day, five days a week. They helped me to better prepare myself for life's challenges as a homeowner.

The brand-new, brick home consists of a garage, four bedrooms, and two bathrooms. I was so looking forward to that day. As the days drew closer, I was getting more and more excited, as I had been dreaming for a long time about owning my own home.

We had some final details to take care of, including finalizing the papers that would allow my husband and I to become a homeowner. These transactions are called "closing." The papers are as thick as a book and we had to sign each one, which took about an hour. Then they congratulated us and gave us the keys. This was the final moment. We were so happy and ready to move.

It took us seven hours to move from a two-bedroom into a four-bedroom home. By the time we finished moving, we were exhausted. Often, a person doesn't know what he has until he has to move it to a new location. We were blessed to have some relatives come from Dallas to help us. Next time I move, I will hire some professional movers.

Chapter Forty-Six
Buying a Car

Everything was going so well in my life. I was in love and Jesus had blessed us with a new home. We still had a few small problems that needed to be addressed. My old car was having some minor problems and I really didn't want to get a new one, but Lee seemed to think that I should! I ended up trading my car for a new one without thinking it through, and that was a big mistake. On top of that, Lee wanted another car, too. Because we acted without thinking it through or consulting our Lord and Savior, we got into major debt. Before you make a major decision, such as buying a car, please make sure that you think things through; because car dealers are out to get you. Make sure that you know the ins and outs of buying a car, including the blue book value. Car dealerships are ready and waiting to take you fast for your money. Believe me, I know; it happened to me too many times.

Chapter Forty-Seven
Getting Into Debt

It was very easy for me to get into debt, even though I took classes not to. It was like an obsession overtook me all at once. I was so excited about buying new things, that I lost complete control.

Impulsive spending overpowered me when I initially settled into my new home. I wanted everything for my new home to be brand new, too. My obsession drove me to buy more and more new furniture. The more I spent, the more I wanted to buy, until the money was gone. I couldn't stop shopping because it really relaxed me. I bought everything that was needed for the house and was very pleased with my accomplishments. I hung the drapes for our eight windows.

We were deep in debt now and owed many people. We acquired so many monthly bills that I had to write them all down on the calendar. So much debt, but the house was beautiful.

Chapter Forty-Eight
My Husband Goes To Jail

We had been in our new home for only around seven months when all hell broke loose. It seemed that my husband was living a double life. He had broken the law.

The police found marijuana in the trunk of his car, so they arrested him on the spot and put him in their police car. Still handcuffed, he escaped from their custody and fled. Meanwhile, at about 2 a.m., the police called me, searching for him. They told me what happened. Lee had been on the run that night for at least five hours.

In the town of Abbott, he asked a store clerk to call me, indicating that his hands were broken. They believed him, because he had wrapped his wrists in a T-shirt, covering the handcuffs. Aware of his escape from the police, I picked him up. Once in the car, he showed me the handcuffs and told me his story. I brought him home. With the handcuffs still on, he took a shower, then a nap.

I was frightened and in shock. I didn't know what to do but turn him in. So I called the police and told them that I would turn my husband in. They told me to bring him in at 6:00 that evening, which I did. The police charged him with escape while in custody and possession of marijuana.

I never expected that my life would change overnight. "The thief cometh not, but for to steal, and to kill and destroy; I come that they might have life, and that they might have it more abundantly" (John 10:10). I thought that I had my life all together. I trusted this man and, all the while, he had been breaking the law. My life was turned upside down.

Chapter Forty-Nine

Depression

Never place all your trust in one person; always place your trust in Jesus, because He will never let you down. He is a friend Who sticks closer than a brother. Proverbs says, "Trust in the Lord with all thy heart, and lean not unto thine own understanding. In all thy ways, acknowledge Him, and He shall direct thy path" (Proverbs 3:5-6).

After my husband's arrest, I was faced with many responsibilities, including all the bills. I really needed to hear from the Lord now. I was so upset about all of it. My husband had changed our lives. Thank God I had a job and church. In church, I found peace and direction. My life had so many problems now. It seemed that life had taken a turn for the worse. I felt depressed and became withdrawn. I felt all alone and abandoned. I also felt embarrassed about the whole thing, because I knew that people were talking about me. My life, at this time, seemed very unstable in every way. I greatly feared losing my husband, my home, and my three cars. I was overcome with fear. A shadow came over my face and all I could do was cry because I was so depressed. I didn't want to visit anyone. I believe that people who do wrong never think of the consequences that their family has to face once they are arrested. It was a very sad time for me. All I wanted to do was hold my head down. For months, I had to answer so many questions from my church family about what took place. They asked questions such as, "Do you still own or did you lose your house?" These questions just kept floating around in my head. It was so hard to stay focused, but I was trying to stand and keep on standing. The process wore me down, because the memories made me sad and fearful.

Yes, time does heal wounds. By the grace of God and through prayer, I managed to pull out of my depressed state. Depression means: "push down, make sad"—and that was me; but Jesus gave me wisdom through it all. I was learning more about myself everyday. I was learning to lean on Jesus a little bit more.

Chapter Fifty
Still Standing

Through all the trials and tribulations that we may face each day, I believe that the way we act in each situation determines how long we stay in the situation. It simply comes down to one issue: are we going to trust God or are we going to trust ourselves? "He that dwelleth in the secret place of the Most High shall abide under the shadow of the Almighty. I will say of the Lord, He is my refuge and my fortress; my God; in Him will I trust" (Psalms 9:1-2).

We must always have power to stand no matter what we go through. We must hold our heads high and know who we are in Jesus Christ. I managed to keep all of my belongings and did not lose the important things, like my sanity. It was Jesus Christ Who held me together, because I placed all my trust in Him. Sometimes, you must let God be God. Someone at church gave me a word at the time; they said that Jesus had given me wisdom, knowledge, and understanding in all the decisions that I had to make. I knew that someone was on my side. I knew that Jesus was and still is the man. I will always trust in Jesus.

Chapter Fifty-One
My Knee Surgery

While my husband was away I started having some problems with my right knee. The diagnosis from the doctor was called "loose bodies," which meant loose pieces of bone. The knee began to give me so much trouble that I had to have surgery.

The X-rays clearly showed that a knee replacement was required; but at the time, I couldn't afford to miss much work, so I had a simple operation. It only required me to miss one month of work. During my recovery after surgery, my son, Teddy, waited on me. He made me TV dinners and church members brought me cooked meals.

The arthritis in my right knee was so severe that I had to undergo more surgery about three years later. I can remember just how infected my knee became the very next day after surgery. I had to go to the doctor so that he could drain the infection off my knee. That was extremely painful. After about two months, I had recovered from the knee surgery.

Because my knee still gave me problems—it ached sometimes—I took pain pills for my knee and lower back. The doctor told me that I would have to have another knee surgery, because my knee had no cartilage left.

Chapter Fifty-Two
My Husband Returns

After serving eleven months, my husband finally returned home from jail, In August of 2006. It was a good day for me. I was very happy. I picked him up from the bus station, and we went home.

The very next day, we went job-hunting and Lee was blessed to get his old job back. What an awesome God we serve! "But my God shall supply all your needs according to His riches in glory by Christ Jesus" (Philippians 4:19). I am living proof that there is a God, because He lives inside of me. He has brought me a mighty long way. He has delivered me from all fear. There is no God like Jehovah.

Now my life was filled with peace again. With my husband's return, we were able to enjoy life again. The struggle of trying to make ends meet from my income alone was a thing of the past.

Chapter Fifty-three

Fighting

My husband loved to drink beer. I felt that he was an alcoholic because he got drunk each and every time he drank. He didn't seem to think that he was one because he only drank on the weekends with his friends and then come home drunk. If he weren't an alcoholic, then why did he get drunk every time? To me, the facts were obvious. The drinking altered his personality. He became argumentative and aggressive with my son and me. Everything had to be done his way.

Three months after Lee returned home, he was back in trouble. He managed to pick a big fight with my son. It lasted at least six hours. My husband had started drinking again and was out of his mind.

But, oh no! We couldn't have this in my house. I told my husband repeatedly to calm down, but he couldn't; so I called his cousins in Dallas to try to calm him down. Lee refused to calm down when they came from Dallas. He wanted to fight everyone who was on his property. I could no longer tolerate his behavior, because it had spiraled out of control. So, I had no choice but to call the police on my husband. While we were waiting for the police to come, Lee kept drinking, speeding off in his car (because he was drunk), going around the block and returning home. I just kept waiting for the police, because I couldn't take it anymore. He was using unacceptable verbal language and causing a big scene. He was totally out of control at this point! I thought that my husband had changed, but oh no! He was still up to his old tricks. He was still crazy!

The police finally arrived on the scene. My son and I explained to them my husband's behavior and they went and talked to him, but he did not want to cooperate. The police asked him what was wrong and he just talked smart to them. So they just arrested him in the house for domestic violence and took him to jail. I felt embarrassed and ashamed. The day after my husband returned from jail, we decided to move him out of the house for a while.

I felt that, at this time, my husband's moving out was for the best. After all, he had started the blow-up with his verbal fighting to begin with. But his leaving left us financially broke. Due to the stress, my life was in turmoil once again. I felt the need to go to church and tell to my sisters and brothers in Christ what had taken place, so that they could pray for me.

Chapter Fifty-Four

Life with an Alcoholic

After about one week, my husband managed to talk me into letting him move back into the house. I still had reservations about him moving back home because he had not changed—he was still drinking.

Life began to improve for the most part. Things were looking good in my marriage. My son was doing well in college and I was very proud of him.

We had a good Christmas in 2007, and now the year 2008 never looked better. I had come through a lot at this point in my life and was able to put the past behind me. After all, the past is the past.

I had vowed that I would never live with an alcoholic because Jesus had delivered me from all fears, including the fear of relapsing into drugs and alcohol. Yet somehow, I managed to marry and live with an alcoholic once again. He could have caused me to relapse!

I didn't believe that I was headed back to hell on earth again, because being around people who drink disgusted me. They emanate a foul odor everywhere they go. There is no way to hide it; I've been there and done that. I had no intention of going back to that kind of life. So I was hoping and praying that my husband would get some help because he was drinking and driving at the same time. He could have had an accident or, worse, been killed or killed someone.

Chapter Fifty-Five
Servant

Meanwhile I was serving God in the most awesome way. I was calling people, praying for them and spending time with some of them. I was walking in the anointing of God and thanking Him that I made it through another year, 2008; because I could have been dead if it wasn't for the Lord.

God had brought me a mighty long way and had set my feet on solid ground. He had given me a good life and my heart's desires, believe me, everything. I stayed focused on Him by putting Him first in all things.

God didn't tell me that the road would be easy; but if I stay focused on Jesus, the author and finisher of my faith, there's not an obstacle that He wouldn't see me through. I have faced trials and tribulation throughout my life, but Jesus said that He would not leave me, that He is my friend and would stick closer than a brother. Jesus called me friend and I am a friend of Jesus. He calls me friend.

Chapter Fifty-Six

Bills and Debts

Once again, I managed to get myself back in debt. Debt is a curse because it prevents you from being able to enjoy life. A few bills are ok, but too many bills were putting me under a big load of stress.

Stress is like a cancer that eats on you a little bit at a time. I loved new things but I hated debt! I wanted to get out of debt real fast, but it's a process; because I didn't get into debt overnight and I wouldn't get out overnight either.

I had developed the most helpful economic strategy to pay my bills and get out of debt. It was to stop spending. If I didn't have the money, I did without the merchandise. It's easier to say than it was to do, especially when I saw a new purse, shoes, or dress that I really wanted and just had to have. *Not* so! I discovered that I didn't have to have it if it wasn't a true necessity. I learned to ask myself, "Do you need it or not?" Then, and only then, could I start on the road to becoming debt-free for good. It feels so good to just say *no*!

Chapter Fifty-Seven
Fighting With the Neighbors

It was November of 2008, and all hell had broken loose. My husband managed to start a fight with the neighbors once again.

He had been drinking that day and doing Lord knows what else. He came home, sat down to eat, and started talking out of his head. He started making negative comments about the house, such as, "This house is a cave." It was the house we were living in and his comments just didn't make sense. I just tried to overlook his behavior, but my son noticed that he was acting differently. Teddy asked him to move his car so that he could leave, so Lee went out to move his car. After a long while, I noticed that he hadn't returned. I went outside and saw him getting into a fight with the neighbors. "Here we go again," I thought. "More violence." Neighbors from one side were trying to stop him from fighting our neighbors on the other side. I was shocked, so I grabbed my husband from behind and helped him into the house. He was still extremely angry and full of alcohol and marijuana. Before leaving for church, I told him not to start any trouble. I warned him that, if he continued his behavior, it was over between us. Meanwhile, the neighbors had called the police. That spooked him, so he suddenly ran out of the house for fear that the law was coming after him.

I left for church because I had a meeting to go to. All the time I was in church, I was so worried about Lee that I had to confide in someone at the meeting. I asked a close friend to pray for me because I was going through something with my husband. I told her what had happened and she proceeded to pray for me.

Immediately after she prayed, I went home. I arrived home to complete chaos. My neighbors met me in my yard and informed me about what had taken place. She explained that my husband had returned with two other men and had started a fight with the neighbors again. She also said that she planned to have him removed from our property. I wondered, "How is that possible?"

I noticed that my mailbox was completely caved in, the result of the physical violence, I found out later.

I was shocked by what my neighbor had told me. I was at a loss for words. The only thing that I could do was apologize, which I did.

I managed to get myself together to call the place where he had driven to after the fight. He was drunk and laughing about the whole thing. I never expected my life to spiral out of control. I knew that life had its ups and downs, but to pick a violent fight with the neighbors was, to me, life in complete chaos.

I had no choice but to ask my husband to move out. Oh boy, was he angry at me for that! He called me some very obscene words that I will not write down in this book. They were very obscene. But coming from bad character, what did I expect, good words?

My husband likes drama in his life, but I don't like it. I like joy and peace. I found out later who won the fight. It was the neighbors. They beat him down to the ground while his friends watched and laughed at him.

After my husband moved out, my son and I had some peace again. A blessed tranquility filled our house.

Three weeks later, I allowed Lee to move back in and the trouble started all over again. He brought trauma and chaos, and I did not sign up for this. I felt that I was a caring person who loved people and animals. I also *like* animals, but people? They are a completely different story. Most people demand attention all the time!

Chapter Fifty-Eight
My Dog

Animals are so gentle and kind. They do what you say all the time, especially dogs. I like dogs. I had a dog named Venca for a few months. She loved to run in the house and play with the stuffed animals. When the front door opened, she would run outside and down the street. It was hard to catch her once she got outside. We would call her and run after her, but she kept on running. The only way we could get her back in the yard was to offer her food. Dogs love food. We later gave the dog away because she was too wild.

Chapter Fifty-Nine
Life Takes a Turn

I was in a very unhappy state of mind. My marriage had gone sour and my health was deteriorating. My husband and I were arguing all the time and didn't even sleep in the same room. We had nothing in common. I loved going to church. He did not. I loved to fellowship with other married people. He did not.

At this time in my life, I was disabled, but still worked two days a week at the restaurant. It was difficult to stand and walk for long periods of time. I needed to sit constantly because of my knee pain. If it had not been for my medication, I don't think that I would have been able to make it to work at all. I was working on getting a disability status from Social Security, and that takes time because you have to be denied by Social Security three times before you can hire a lawyer to represent your case. Your disability must be serious, or they won't take your case. I am glad that I found a lawyer to take mine. Meanwhile, we had so many bills coming in each month, and I felt that I wasn't pulling my share of the load. My husband felt that I was faking my disability to get out of working. But that was not true at all. The Lord knew my pain; He knew. I did feel that it was time to get a knee replacement, because my lower back was in constant pain. My right knee also hurt constantly, due to arthritis and the absence of cartilage. The summer of 2010, I planned to have surgery on my right knee. That way, I would be able to walk normally, because right now, I walk with a limp. I don't mind walking with a limp because I just can't help it. I just don't want anyone to feel sorry for me and say, "Poor, Cy; she's walking with a limp and has to wait on tables." I am a people-person and I love to work with the public. People inspire me, especially older people. They have a great sense of humor. They are always smiling and show up at the restaurant every single day. I like old people because they are so friendly and kind. Every now and then, I ran into a mean old person and they could be real mean at the restaurant. But for the most part, they were so kind and friendly and full of love.

Chapter Sixty
The Pain Doctor

As I said I walked with a limp. On the second of December, I was scheduled to see a pain doctor. I was not looking forward to this visit at all, because I had heard some terrible stories about the doctor.

I arrived on time to see the pain doctor, only to find out for myself what kind of a doctor he was. I told him my medical history along with my family problems, too. I shouldn't have done that, because he said some unkind things about my disability. He said that I wasn't disabled any way and shouldn't apply for my social security. That turned out to be my worst doctor's appointment ever. The doctor was unprofessional, mean, and evil. He insisted that I stop the pain medication immediately and start getting shots in my knee as soon as possible. He felt that this would be the best way to help the pain in my knee and back. He said that I was taking too much medication and ordered my family physician to discontinue the medicine called hydrocodone that I was currently taking.

Chapter Sixty-One
The Pain Medication

Hydrocodone is a substitute for Vicodine, and the pain doctor may have thought that I had become addicted to this medication. Of course, I was upset with the doctor when I left his office, because he wanted to stick needles in my knee and back! I couldn't believe that he could be so harsh and insensitive to patients and continue to practice as a physician. Oh well, life goes on.

I wanted to prove to myself that I wasn't addicted to the pain medication. So I stopped the hydrocodone, put myself to the test, and won. I was not addicted to pain medication because my Jesus delivered me from all addictions. The Bible says, 2 Timothy 4:18, "And the Lord shall deliver me from every evil work, and will preserve me unto His heavenly kingdom: to Whom be glory forever and ever." Amen. May God bless the pain doctor and give him peace.

Chapter Sixty-Two
Christmas 2008

Christmas is the best time of the year for me. It was Christmas of 2008, and it was wonderful. I received the most beautiful gifts ever. I received two purses, two pairs of socks, a glass cross, a tweed jacket, a blouse, a Lexmark printer, a mug of candy, an egg glass plate, one small bottle of body lotion, and a pair of beautiful birthstone earrings.

Christmas is our celebration of the birth of Christ. Jesus truly is the reason for the season. Without Christ, there is no Christmas; without Christ, there is no life for me. Jesus said, "I am the vine, ye are the branches; He that abideth in Me, and I in him, the same bringeth forth much fruit: for without me ye can do nothing" (John 15:5). I can't do anything without Jesus Christ; therefore; I will abide in him forever.

Many people say that they are Christians, but do their own thing. Some of them are quick to quote Scriptures to create a "holier than thou" image. Beware of people who know everything about the Bible, and yet refuse to receive correction or counsel of any kind.

Chapter Sixty-Three
My Son's Early Adult Years

My son was now twenty years old and was a good kid. I say this because I raised him as a single parent. He was in his second year of college, pursuing a degree in business. Teddy said that although the classes were difficult, he was studying hard. He not only passed all his classes; he was also still active in church, in the music department. During the Christmas holiday, Teddy started his first job ever at Wal-Mart. He liked his job and planned to continue working and going to school. I was so proud of my son, Teddy.

He has his own car, which is paid for and because it's his first vehicle, he loves it very much. Soon after he bought the car, he had his first accident. He ran into the back of his best friend's car. I believe that he made a very careless mistake, but accidents occur very frequently among teenagers.

Chapter Sixty-Four
A New President

I started a new recovery plan to get out of debt and, most of the time, it was working. I usually bought only what I needed, not what I wanted. It's a process.

Life was going well at this time. Our country had just elected the first African-American president and we were all excited. He is for change. We needed change because the Republican Party had messed up the economy. Many people had lost their jobs; the number was in the millions.

This was the last month in 2008 and life here in the United States was difficult. There were a lot of major companies closing and people just didn't know how to make ends meet; but thank God for Jesus. He is the author and finisher of our faith. He will always come through for us if we believe in Him. I believe that God allows things to happen so that we can draw closer to Him.

I had asked Jesus to let Barak Obama become president. During the vote count, I sensed the Holy Spirit telling me that Obama would win the election. Obama's becoming president brought a shift in the atmosphere for African-Americans.

The year 2009 started off very positive not only for me, but for the whole nation. We now had the first African-American president in the White House, Barak Obama. He is very intelligent and is also a Democrat.

He planned to correct the $825 billion national deficit with an economic stimulus bailout because it was bad to carry on with the Bush administration's economic plan. The Republican Party managed to turn the world upside down. People in the USA and in other countries lost their jobs due to the slumped economy. President Barak Obama plans to use the bailout to help the economy.

Bailout, bailout; that was all it had been about these days. Large banks and the auto industry had been bailed out. What about the working class who owe so much money to the banks? I, too, was still deep in debt and needed a bailout.

Chapter Sixty-Five

Another Crisis – My Husband's Arrest

The New Year (of 2009) came in with a bang. A big bang! I arrived home from my church's New Year's Eve service shortly after midnight, to discover that my husband was not at home.

The next morning, New Year's Day, Gracie, the wife of my husband's best friend, came over to inform me that my husband had gotten arrested three minutes before the New Year and was in jail. She went on to explain that he had railed a police car. "What!" I exclaimed. I felt like I was in the Twilight Zone. Things had to change!

Gracie said that he needed someone to pick him up from jail. I told her that I couldn't do it, because I had to go to work. Even though it was New Year's Day, I still had to work.

I did a great job at work that day and then went home. Because I had prepared dinner the night before, all I had to do was heat it up. Around 10 p.m. my husband came home, after bonding himself out of jail, to tell me about the arrest. Of course, it was never his fault when he told the story.

I listened patiently to his story. He said that the police had pulled him over for no reason. He felt that they had pulled him over because he was a black man in a new car. He claimed that they were prejudiced against him. I came to a decision that he is an alcoholic who is in denial. This denial is the type of behavior that causes family members to get stressed and to break down. If the marriage was going to work, he must change and get help because marriage is a give-and-take relationship. Each must give and take; but some take too much.

Why keep doing the same things and making the same mistakes over and over again? Why keep breaking the law? Why? I don't understand why anyone who is in his right frame of mind does not want to change his destructive behavior. One definition of insanity is "Doing the same thing over and over again and expecting a different result." There are so many resources out there to help people with their addictions. All we have to do is ask Jesus to come into our heart and help us change.

I believe that some people don't want to change. Lee wanted to continue in his wicked ways, just doing his own thing. He cared only about having fun, about partying, drinking, and doing drugs. He said that it relaxed him and made him happy. Yet, when Lee got into trouble, he always looked very sad. He made comments of regret, such as, "I shouldn't have drank so much," or "I spent too much money and I don't know where it went to."

Chapter Sixty-Six
How Alcohol Rules

I had come to realize that alcoholics are sometimes foolish. They continue to make the same mistakes. They do not pay attention to the serious problems of the disease and the effects that it has on the individual or the family. The family of an alcoholic suffers fear at all times. I lived in constant fear, while being married to Lee, because I was always worried about him drinking and driving. Lee was a good husband who worked very hard to provide for his family, but when he came under the influence of alcohol, he always changed. The evil inside him would come out and alter his capacity to think and would influence everything that he did and said. I could see the visible change. That's why I was so afraid for him to drink and drive. He wasn't afraid, but I was afraid for him.

A few days passed and I believed that everything was going to be all right. I thought, "Surely, this couldn't be happening again." One week went by and guess what happened? My husband was arrested for a parole violation. I couldn't believe that this could happen twice in a marriage. Where was the limit? Was there no stopping point? When would the problems stop? I don't understand how someone can allow himself or herself to continue to get put in jail. This grown man was acting like a little boy. He couldn't stop getting into trouble. And guess what? I got tired of picking up the pieces in our marriage. I did not sign up for this. This arrest didn't have to happen. We were blessed with so many things and he was not satisfied. I wanted him to be careful, but he just wouldn't listen to me. He said, "You're a Christian and you talk too much."

Chapter Sixty-Seven
A Changed Life

My life changed after my husband's arrest. It felt like a death had taken place in my life. How does one prepare for something like this? We didn't have any savings and debt collectors were calling us way before my husband was arrested.

Now the phone was about to ring off the receiver. Wells Fargo (bank) was calling many times everyday about the car. I didn't know what to tell them. I couldn't afford the car. All I could do now was what I had always done. When trouble or chaos occurred, I called on the Son of the Living God, Jesus. "Jesus, help me please!"

At this time, I owned three cars. I had to stand on my faith and pray for a miracle from God. I had faith. Hebrews 11:1 says, "Faith is the substance of things hoped for, the evidence of things not seen." I believe that Jesus would set me on solid ground, restore my mind, and give me peace.

Chapter Sixty-Eight

Depending on God Alone

Now, I was single once again and relying on myself and God to pull me out of this debt mess. In times like these, I had to trust and rely on a power stronger and greater than myself.

No one is going to just drop some money into your lap. You're going to have to work and stand in faith, believing that you will receive. I'm going to stay strong in God, just trusting Him because, Philippians 4:19 says, "But my God shall supply all your needs according to His riches in glory by Christ Jesus." It's very hard sometimes to trust in God and not your own husband or yourself, but God's Word never returns void. In order for faith to work, you must believe in His word.

It had been three days since my husband was arrested and life was very difficult, but I knew that I was going to make it once again because my mind was getting clear again. I could think things through without feeling pressured to make decisions that I knew would backfire on me. I was taking one day at a time now.

Chapter Sixty-Nine
Being Humble

I found that it is all right to be a little sad or depressed, as long as you don't let it consume you. It's all right to cry out to the Lord and ask Him to help you through anything that may have bound or depressed you. That is what He is here for, to help you. He is closer to you than you will ever know. So I cried out to Him and went to church and prayed at the altar. That turned out to be a major blessing because some of the people there could relate to my pain and gave me some encouraging words. Their counsel and encouragement helped me a lot. The most important part of going through a trial is to be open and honest with yourself and with someone who you can trust. Don't put your trust in just anyone—only in those who are called by God. I went to church that day to seek a major breakthrough in my life. I needed to be set free from some harmful attitudes that had attached themselves to me spiritually and taken root inside of me. The two main attitudes were unforgiveness and guilt. I had to forgive.

I needed to forgive my husband for leaving me broke, because I had very little money at the time and no longer had good health insurance. I also needed to forgive myself for feeling guilty. The guilt took root because for a while I believed that if I had made it from church on time on New Year's Eve, as I had promised, he wouldn't have gone out like he did. I felt that his arrest was my fault. God removed those harmful roots from me as I asked people at church to pray for me. Church gave me a whole lot of peace of mind. Sometimes, you need to go and get God's rest and reassurance and to lay things down at the cross.

Chapter Seventy

I Found Peace in God

My life had been filled with stress and chaos but now I found much peace. There were many worries swimming around in my head before my husband's arrest such as, "How am I going to make it without my husband's income?" Now, I'm happy, at peace, and full of joy. "The joy of the Lord is your strength" (Nehemiah 8:10). There had been a dark cloud hanging over me while I was with my alcoholic husband; but now I could see the sun and it was good to be alive and enjoy life. Life does come at you fast; are you ready?

I have found in my walk with God that I must stay prayed up and ready, because the devil comes in like a flood. He walks around like a lion. He is no lion; he just acts like one. If he finds that you are weak in any area, then he attacks that area. For this reason, you must stay prayed up.

Christians must come together and pray for one another and lift each other up in love. This is how the world knows that we are Christians, by our love for each other. This love makes us peculiar people.

Sometimes, being a Christian is difficult; but it is so rewarding. I know, when I take my last breath, where my spirit will go. For now however, I am here on Earth to make a difference in someone's life. I try to sow seeds everywhere I go. I encourage and compliment people as much as I can with a smile on my face. Some people ask me,"Why do you smile all the time?" I respond by saying, "Because I have Jesus in the inside."

Chapter Seventy-One
Collection Agency and Phone Calls

Phone calls and more phone calls. I just let it keep ringing. All they wanted was money that I didn't have. They called all day long, asking the same questions: "When are you going to make a payment and how much?" Sometimes, it seemed like I was the only one on their list. It made me angry that they harassed me so much! You can't give something you don't have. I told the collectors that I was disabled and that my husband was arrested. Their response was simple: "What does that have to do with us? We just need our money or the car."

I looked to Jesus and told Him that I needed a miracle in my finances at this time in my life. Now, I had to stand on my faith. I knew the collection agency phone calls were not going to stop in one day; but I believed that by trusting in God, I would eventually get my debts paid off. I was at His mercy and knew He would work it out.

Chapter Seventy-Two
My New Roommate

My husband's second incarceration left me in a financial bind, almost broke really. But I always kept my faith in God! So I decided to rent out a room in my house. The guest room, as a matter of fact. I tried placing an ad in the newspaper for a roommate, but got no response. The ad stated, "Christian female only." Then, I spoke to my long-time friend, Sue, about the room for rent and she said yes!

I first met Sue at church years before, when she had serious medical problems. She had some disabilities that prevented her from living a normal life. Sue was born almost totally deaf, so she wore a hearing aid. She was a very strong woman! She also lost her sight in one eye in the streets. I chose Sue for a roommate because I was desperate at the time. We set up a monthly rent for $325.00. We both agreed and it was settled. We were so excited. I was also looking forward to having fellowship, since my life had been kind of isolated and boring.

It took her a long time to move in because she had so much stuff. I came home one day and found my garage full of boxes and different things that looked like they were from the 1960s and '70s. It looked like a yard sale. She had shoes, dishes, clothes, and furniture. I could not believe the stuff that she had accumulated and hoarded! When I saw the room, I was shocked. There was barely enough room for her to get from her bed to the door. It was as though she never threw anything away. I just had to adjust to my new roommate and tenant, per say.

Things got off to a reasonable start for us. We hung out and I would usually take her shopping when she asked me to because I still had my part-time job. Sue would always cook dinner, since my son and I always worked, and she was at home with nothing to do all day. At least, that's what I thought. One thing's for sure, you never really know someone until you live with him or her. Sue would cook dinner and wait all day to eat. Then, when we arrived home from work, we would all eat except Sue; so we assumed that she had already eaten. When we finished eating, she would get very, very angry with us and accuse us of eating all the food. This pattern went on for about a week. I had finally had enough and decided that we should each buy our own food from then on.

One night, after arguing about the meal, I heard someone crying out, "Help me! Help me!" The voice was coming from Sue's room. Upon entering, I saw that she was gasping for air. She was in the middle of an asthma attack. I quickly helped her assemble the oxygen equipment and mask. She soon calmed down and I went back to my room.

Her behavior continued to arouse suspicions in me. What I didn't know at the time was that Sue had an alternate personality. I found out that there were a lot of things about herself that she was hiding. She was, in fact, an alcoholic and chain smoker. While I was at work, everyday she would go back and forth to the store with her caregiver, buying cigarettes, 40 ounces of beer, and lottery tickets. I didn't find out about this hidden lifestyle until one day, when I was emptying the trash, I discovered some beer bottles and lottery tickets. I knew they were hers, not my son's because I could smell the alcohol on her breath. I didn't know how to approach her about my findings because, after all, she was a grown woman and paying rent.

As time went on, she complained more and more. She would fly into a rage against me and then storm into the kitchen. After Sue had moved out, I found out that while I had been at work, she often went walking through the neighborhood, talking and texting to her friends on her cell phone. I was the topic of the conversations. She acted like I was the bad person. After she had spent all her income, she started pressuring me, stating that I charged her too much for rent.

One couple that she often talked to about me came to visit her quite often. They were close friends with her. At the time, I didn't notice very much because I was in and out, attending church services; but I did notice that the couple would stay with her in the room a long time with the door closed. So I gave them their privacy. I found out later that she was no friend to the couple, because she was having a sexual relationship with the woman's husband while braiding his hair.

One day, my friend Morris asked me if I could pick him up from work, and I said yes. Then, we stopped by my house to pick up a grocery list because after dropping him off, I planned on going to the store. As we pulled into my driveway, Morris asked me, "Who is that white man parked in your driveway?" I said that I didn't know, so we asked the man who he was looking for, and he replied, "Sue." The gentleman was very upset because he wanted the money for the marijuana that she had smoked up. Seeing that Morris and I were not drug users, the man left.

I was sure that Sue had smoked the marijuana in the house. At this point, I was in shock. Here I was, providing her a place to stay, and she had totally taken control of my house. Sue wasn't the friend whom I thought she was when I let her move into my house. It turned out that she was partying and having all kinds of company while we were at work. This was the last straw! I had no choice but to confront her.

She got very upset with me and told me that I owed her $3.00 and demanded that I pay her at once. I refused and she became extremely angry with me. Within a few minutes, her personality had changed so much that I could no longer recognize her. She had apparently switched to one of her alternate personalities, talking like a street bully. She went outside, and I followed her. Because of her bullying, I lost my cool. I was no longer going to allow Sue to control me or my home, because we were Christians and I thought that she was, too. I believe that the evil spirits were already in her and in the house at that point. That scene happened outside.

We went back into the house, and things got very ugly at that point. A jealous spirit suddenly manifested in her, a very nasty spirit. I could no longer take her verbal abuse, so I ordered her to get her things and leave at once. She refused, saying that her rent was paid.

She approached me in the hallway, drunk as usual, and shouted that her friends (the couple) said that she was paying too much rent. (She made that comment only because she had been loaning them money.) All this was happening while my friend Morris was visiting. I was so upset and angry by all the name-calling, arguing, and accusing, that I jumped into my flesh and put on my tennis shoes, thinking, "You never know what a person under the influence of drugs might do."

There we were, in the hallway. She had a hammer, so I picked up a knife. It was wrong, but I had to defend myself in my home, since she was now moving aggressively toward me. At that point, Morris jumped between us and prevented a disaster from happening.

After he stopped the fight, she went outside and called the police on me, in my house! Can you believe it? I called her two friends to come remove her from my house.

When the police arrived, they talked to me first. I told them that she was out of control, like a madwoman. They took her in the house, walked her to her room, and told her to get her stuff and leave. They weren't playing around because, at one point, when she took too long (about an hour), the police hit her. We heard her holler.

I was extremely relieved that the cops got her out that day. She was a handful. My life became tranquil and pleasant again, now that she was out of my house. (That rat!) What a roommate she was. I will never ever forget Sue. But I forgave her in Jesus' name. And I pray that Jesus will change her life and renew her mind for the glory of God, because He is not the author of confusion.

Chapter Seventy-Three
Medical Problems

I got sick recently and thought that I could treat the systems with over-the-counter medicine, but it didn't work. I had to seek medical attention. The doctor diagnosed me with a lung infection and placed me on antibiotics along with cough medicine. I was so ill that I had lost my voice; but I continued to work and support my family.

It was quite a challenge taking the cough medicine, because it made me feel sleepy all the time and like I was walking on clouds. I wasn't myself at all. My joy was gone, but I continued to take the medication as prescribed once every six hours.

I was glad that the medication took effect so that I could speak clearly and feel like my old self again. I was truly relieved that my illness wasn't worse than it was. It was not a good feeling to be sick.

Chapter Seventy-Four

It's a New Year

It was a new year—2010—and things were going just fine, because I was taking it one day at a time. I couldn't worry about the bills, food, and clothing. The Lord said to take one day at a time.

I was feeling stronger since I had been by myself, more responsible and aware of life. Life can pass you by if you let it. Just stay focused on being happy and attending church regularly; that's what I was doing.

We were in a recession at this time, but Texas was holding its own and so was I. I was working two and a half days a week now and liked that better than staying at home, because work is truly good for the soul.

I don't understand how people could stay at home and not work; I would get bored. I guess they feel that they deserve to stay at home because of all the hours that they had worked over the years. Whatever! I just can't stay at home everyday and not get out and do something.

Chapter Seventy-Five
My Good Life

Things are finally looking good for me now because I was able to get rid of junk in my life. I do realize that life is what we make of it. It's really up to the individual to choose to have a blessed life. God's best life! Storms will come and go because that's a part of life that we have no control over. But no matter what, we must always stand for the Lord, because He is always there in times of trouble. I know this is true! My life is very good now and I have overcome many of my fears because the Lord Jesus is always by my side. Through it all I've learned to depend on Jesus, the author and finisher of my faith. I'm having no problems with the collection agencies. I pay them on time, so there is no phone call that I can't handle. Life is so good now. I filed for a divorce and it was done within three months. The judge gave me the house and the car. The car was mine anyway.

I don't have one complaint against my life at this time. My only regret is that I've never located my son's father in Houston, Texas. I've learned to enjoy life! I was able to receive social security by the grace of God. Now, my life is more complete. I do believe that, because God gave us all a free will, we sometimes can make some bad choices in life. However, it's truly up to the individual to correct his mistakes. There's only one perfect person that I know of, and that is God Himself. So we all have sinned and fallen short of God's glory. (Rom. 3:23)

Thank you so much for taking the time to read my life story. I hope you were blessed!